Life Lessons from My Five-Year-Old

Life Lessons from My Five-Year-Old

My Five-Year-Old

Recognizing the Moments That Matter

Kimber Lynne

iUniverse, Inc.
Bloomington

LIFE LESSONS FROM MY FIVE-YEAR-OLD
RECOGNIZING THE MOMENTS THAT MATTER

iUniverse books may be ordered through booksellers or by contacting:

iUniverse
1663 Liberty Drive
Bloomington, IN 47403
www.iuniverse.com
1-800-Authors (1-800-288-4677)

Because of the dynamic nature of the Internet, any web addresses or links contained in this book may have changed since publication and may no longer be valid. The views expressed in this work are solely those of the author and do not necessarily reflect the views of the publisher, and the publisher hereby disclaims any responsibility for them.

Any people depicted in stock imagery provided by Thinkstock are models, and such images are being used for illustrative purposes only.

Certain stock imagery © Thinkstock.

ISBN: 978-1-4759-6942-9 (sc)
ISBN: 978-1-4759-6940-5 (e)

Library of Congress Control Number: 2012924187

Printed in the United States of America

iUniverse rev. date: 1/24/2013

To my friends and family, thank you for all your support over the years as I have searched for that "something more" in my life. To my daughter, you are truly my greatest gift and most important teacher, and I love you with all my heart. You brighten my world and everyone you touch by being who you really are and by spreading the knowledge you instinctively know from your very old and wise soul.

Table of Contents

Preface

THIS BOOK IS ABOUT REMEMBERING and reconnecting with what matters most to you. In this book I will share part of my journey to become who I have always wanted to be! Sometimes you need to be reminded of the basic things so that you can enjoy your life instead of just existing. I have learned that it's about making choices and recognizing the moments in life that matter most that help define who you are and who you want to be.

I have been searching for something my entire life. Over the past few years, I have taken the time to really look at myself and find my voice. What I discovered is that I have a lot to say and that my conduit for finding my words is my daughter. She is the most important person in my life, and I am so fortunate to be her mom. I waited a long time to become a parent and, through persistence and working through the system, was able to adopt her after a long and arduous process.

It is through my daughter's observations of life that I have reconnected with who I am and what I want in life. Now when I look in the mirror I no longer see an empty shell of my former self, but rather the excitement and anticipation of what is still to come. I have used quotes from my daughter at the beginning of most chapters as my starting point for each life lesson. It is these observations that have helped me to remember what I most care about and to work through some of my thoughts and attitudes that I don't want to pass on to her.

Because writing this book has had such a powerful effect on my life, I am willing to expose my strengths and weaknesses to all of you. My hope is that this book will be your inspiration to begin your own personal exploration and make changes that will impact your life in a meaningful way.

We are all just works in progress, and I continue to work on being in the moment every day. What I can say with all honesty is that I *am* making progress and so can you!

Introduction: Who Are You ... Really?

WHAT DOES THAT MEAN: WHO are you really? It's about understanding who each of us is at our very core, our essence, who we want and choose to be. It's a powerful thing to awaken, acknowledge, and unleash what you know you were born to do. I believe that we all know what our calling or purpose is, and the question is when will we choose to awaken, acknowledge, and act on it. For a number of years, I have had this sense that there was something more in life that I am supposed to achieve. I've been unable to articulate what it was or what to do with it, until now.

As I look back over my life, key moments begin to reveal themselves. I remember having drinks with a friend a few years ago when I was in Kansas City for Christmas visiting my family. This particular friend is someone I have known since we were in junior high, which is more years ago than I care to admit. I now live in New York City, which is a very different way of life than in Kansas City, where we grew up. He made an interesting comment to me that was absolutely dead-on. He said that as long as he could remember, I had always been searching for something more, different, bigger, better and had never really seemed content. In stark contrast, he didn't want anything more than he had. We had two completely different approaches to life, and yet neither of us was right or wrong. We just saw the world very differently.

His observation of me was absolutely right, but at the time I saw it as negative. It's true: I have been searching for something my entire life. I didn't know what that "more" was then, but I knew it was out there waiting for me to discover it. There was a force far bigger than me that continued to push me to take risks even though I didn't know what the outcome would be. Some of the risks I have taken have definitely come with a price, but the sum of the whole makes me realize that each step along the journey continued to move me to where I am today. Over the years, my longtime friend and spiritual advisor Ruby has reinforced with me that we are all exactly where we need to be in this moment in time for our greatest growth and development. My translation is that it has taken all these years and life experiences to get me to where I am and to know what I need to know right now. My greatest desire is to share those experiences with you and, hopefully, motivate and inspire all of you to live life to its greatest and fullest potential.

Last year, I attended a work-related breakfast and heard a senior executive speak. I would say it was the right message at the right time for me. His message was about "knowing your truth," and he posed these questions: "Do you know your truth? Are you living it, or are you on the path to living it? And if not, how do you get there?" I thought a lot about those words that were so impactful to me that day. Know your truth. What did that mean exactly? For some reason, by his asking that question, I felt I had been given permission to answer the question honestly. I mean really honestly. What I discovered was that I actually know exactly who I am, what I can and should be doing, and what I want out of life. I just hadn't ever given myself permission before to say it out loud, let alone to figure out how to make it a reality.

So how do I boil down into one statement what my truth is? My truth or the path I am to follow is centered around motivating and inspiring the human spirit both for myself and for those I come in contact with. So what exactly does that mean? I think my truth breaks down into three parts.

Part One: Motivating Others

What makes people tick, and how can they be motivated not only for a productive work environment but to achieve what they want personally? Getting to know what people value and care about allows you to better understand and connect with them. To be a true leader personally and professionally, it is about seeing the bigger picture, all of the components, focusing on your strengths and those of others.

Part Two: Inspiring Others

It is important to understand what inspires you as well as others. Where does your inspiration come from, and how can you fulfill what your heart needs to keep you on the right path? How do you bring yourself back to what you already know to be true in order to feel inspired and gain enjoyment from normal, everyday experiences?

Part Three: Being Enveloped in the Human Spirit

What I am continually learning or relearning from my five-year-old daughter is probably the most important part of all. Here's what I know for sure. My eyes, and more importantly my heart, have opened up to the possibilities and lessons I have needed to learn or remember. It is because of her that I have been able to move from a place of fear and just getting through the everyday grind, to a place where my heart is open and the truth and reality of who I am has begun to surface. I have no greater teacher than my five-year-old, and all of the thoughts and ideas I will share are her gifts to you.

Chapter 1: To Risk or Not to Risk, That Was My Question

"I was just completely over myself and knew there had to be a bigger purpose to my life."

—Kimber, Age 38

LET ME START BY TELLING you a little about how I got to where I am today. I am from the Midwest and led a very traditional life, but as far back as I can remember, I was always searching for something different, never feeling content with anything in my life: not the city I lived in, not the job I had, not the life I was living.

At age thirty-eight, I took one of the biggest risks I have ever taken; I left everything and everyone I had ever known in Kansas City and moved to New York City. I knew that I needed a change in a big way, but was moving to New York a rational decision? Probably not, but that didn't stop me. I took a job that I knew wasn't going to be right for me, but something inside of me said it was now or never if I had any hope of changing the outcome of my life. So I will state the obvious that, of course, I could have changed my life in many ways staying where I was. The rational side of my brain was on a temporary sabbatical when I made this life-altering decision. I packed my bags, left my little house on the prairie, and headed for the Big Apple. This move took me down a path of many big risks to follow, and even though I was absolutely miserable for months, there was something inside of me that would not give up. I was searching for that "something more," not knowing what it was or if I would find it.

Now this is not at all uncommon for any of us, to feel like we need to shake things up and make some kind of change in our lives. I have one friend who knew what her path was much earlier in life. She was completely aware of what was working and what wasn't. I love how courageous she was to drastically change her life in an instant. She was an officer at a bank; it was a great job with good upward mobility. One day, right before her thirtieth birthday, she was sitting at a meeting with all of the officers of the bank, and a question was posed to everyone at the table. When they got around to her for her input, she answered a very different question. She said, "You know, I just don't want to wear pantyhose to work anymore." Her coworkers were dumbfounded by her seemingly bizarre response. Later that week she chose to leave that job and pursue other options. What clarity and courage she had at a relatively young age to know that she needed to make a change and to follow through to make it a reality!

My clarity came much later in life. My first three years in New York City were filled with so much turmoil—multiple changes in jobs, 9/11, and yet another bad relationship that was going nowhere. Oh, and by the way, my fortieth birthday was right around the corner.

I had many moments of thinking there must be something more or a much bigger purpose for my existence, and over the years I'd had some glimmers of what that could be, yet nothing really gelled for me. I then landed a stable job at a great company, moved to Connecticut, ended the latest bad relationship, and thought to myself, *Okay, now what?*

I had several friends who had gotten married to men who had children from previous relationships and decided they didn't want any more kids. I thought to myself, *No one gets to make that decision for me. If I get into another relationship it's going to be a package deal.* That is the moment I made the decision to pursue adoption. Adoption? As a single parent? Was I nuts?

"I was just completely over myself and knew there had to be a bigger purpose to my life."

There were many times over the next three years during the adoption process that made me question the decision. I went through a really big "poor me" phase, where I thought that if I moved forward with adoption I was admitting to myself that I would never get married. Ridiculous, I know, but again, back to the rational brain thing, which wasn't always working for me. I questioned myself constantly, and yet something far bigger than me kept pushing me forward in the process, in spite of all of the obstacles I continued to face.

My family and friends had a beautiful baby shower for me. The odd thing about the day was that I attended my baby shower and then attended the high school graduation of a good friend's son on the same day. That was a little bit of a reality check on my age. In case you haven't been keeping track, I was now in my early forties and clearly old enough to have a son or daughter in college, not in diapers. I wondered if my daughter's friends were going to ask whether I was her mom or her grandmother. That thought was definitely not appealing.

To make matters worse, I had a challenging adoption experience, with delay after delay. After three years in paperwork and constant uncertainty, I can honestly tell you that most people would have quit. I continued to hang in there, even though it was an emotional roller coaster. I don't know which was worse, having people ask me on a daily basis when my daughter was coming home or having to tell them I didn't know.

I got the first picture of my daughter when she was only six weeks old, and it was magical, overwhelming, amazing, and terrifying all at the same time. And then it was during my first trip to visit her, when she was around four months old, that I started to become aware of the challenges that were ahead. What I didn't realize then was how hard the road was going to be. The biggest issue was that there was a challenge with one of the birth mother's documents, which began the spiral. I had no control over it and had to work within the system, completely relying on my adoption agency and their contacts in another country. I got updated photos once a month and would travel to stay with my daughter for just a weekend at a time. I ultimately made four trips to her country over almost nineteen months before finally being able to bring her home. Every time I visited her and realized how much I was missing, and with an unknown end date, it was like ripping a little piece of my heart out when I had to leave her with her foster family. Even though I knew she was being well taken care of, missing milestones, like seeing her crawl for the first time, take her first steps, have her first teeth come in, celebrate her first birthday, were all like taking painful hits to my stomach as I waited and worked through the system. Other people I knew during this time got pregnant, gave birth, and went on with their new lives. For me, parenthood was like an invisible, intangible enigma out there that sometimes felt like more of a possibility than a reality. But there was something about this particular little girl that I was waiting to bring home; I knew, beyond a doubt, that we were meant to be together. So I had no other option than to ride it out as long as it took.

I could go on and on about all of my trips to the country where my daughter was born, but would rather just get to a little good news. Enough drama already! I finally got my daughter after years of waiting. It continued to be a challenge as I didn't know how to be a parent of a nineteen-month-old; there are no parent guides to really tell you how to go from being single to having a toddler. Eventually, we got into a good routine, and I can now say undoubtedly it was the best thing I have ever done.

My aha moment was this: I thought it was going to be all about what I could offer her, but instead it has been the complete opposite. She literally saved me from myself and the daily insanity life deals out. She has helped me remember what really matters in life. Life is really all about the series of moments we experience: learning how to be present for really extraordinary moments and how we can learn from our experiences and from other people.

So *to risk or not to risk* certainly was part of my question, and the risks that I took helped me get on the right path. I now understood one part of what my bigger purpose in life was all about. Become a parent … check. Now I am not saying that taking crazy, life-altering risks is right for everyone. I'm just sharing a little peek into the somewhat nontraditional life I have happily created for myself. I knew that being a parent was part of the answer, and a very big part of it. But it was still hanging out there for me—a great big resounding … *What else?* I continued to search for the more that was now to be for both of us. I knew that there was still a larger contribution that I needed and wanted to make.

So here we are today. As a result of my discovery on this ongoing journey, I have pulled together some of the biggest life lessons I have learned from my five-year-old in an attempt to help you connect with the moments that matter most in your life and to help you live the life you are meant to live.

Life Lesson #1 from my five-year-old: All of the risks and emotional hurdles can help move you from the off ramp back onto the main road moving forward. My journey of becoming a parent for this specific adorable little girl was definitely moving me in the right direction.

Put It into Practice: Trust yourself—you already know the answers.

Now do a little life-inventory exercise. Sometimes we have to look at our past to help us better define what is important to us and what direction we want to go in.

- Think about some of the key decisions you have made or not made over a certain period of time. It could be a week, a month, or even the past year. What can you or have you learned by the decisions you made?
- Can you identify two or three obstacles you have overcome and what you gained from going through these situations?

You don't need to have all of the answers just yet. Doing the work to get to know yourself a little better will certainly help kick-start uncovering your truth or passion and bring you more into living in and recognizing the moment you are in right now.

Notes

Notes

Chapter 2: Back to the Basics

—◦⦿⦿◦—

**"You can't change somebody else.
You can only change yourself."**

—B, Age 5

I HAD A LITTLE FUN with my daughter on our walk to swim class one morning. In New York City, where we live, lots of activity goes on around you all of the time. On this particular day, I said to my daughter, "Let's see what we can hear today as we walk down the street." Of course, she started with the obvious sounds of the cars, and the sound of the tires on the wet pavement and driving through the puddles. Then we both listened harder, and we heard some birds and the wind passing through the trees. Now if you live pretty much anywhere other than New York City, you would say, "What is such a big deal about that?" And my response would be, "When was the last time you stopped and actually listened to the sounds of the birds and the wind blowing through the trees?" Just because you *can* doesn't mean you actually *do*.

What did this exercise accomplish for me and my daughter? It brought us into the same moment. We were both completely focused on listening and were in tune with our surroundings. We were in sync and present for each other at that very moment in time. No cell phone. No BlackBerry. No computer. No TV. Isn't that really all we want from other people? For them to be present with us? It doesn't have to be all of the time, and I don't think it even has to be for long periods of time. Just be present and be aware of what's going on around you. Truly experience these moments *together*. By making that conscious shift, I instantly became aware of my surroundings, which then had more meaning.

When was the last time you felt something other than exhausted and overwhelmed? How about the last time you felt real joy or happiness? Seems like a basic question, doesn't it? Hopefully, so many happy moments pop into your mind that you can't narrow it down to just one. But maybe you have to stop and really think about it and still come up with nothing. Lots of things make us happy or content, but recalling them may be challenging, because we are always so busy down in the weeds and details of our daily life that we forget to look up and recognize important moments as they are happening. I know I am guilty of that. The truth is, we have our daily routines and needs that must be met. That takes a lot of energy. Period.

I propose that it is how you choose to manage the routine that makes the difference. I call this getting back to the basics. It isn't about changing everything you do in your life. It isn't saying that your daily routines aren't important or necessary. I am simply saying it is okay to pause and notice some of the extraordinary things that are happening around you in every moment.

You can start by intentionally using all of your senses, which I know sounds pretty basic. For just a few minutes, think about your morning routine: what you do before you even get to work or get the kids to school or whatever makes up your morning schedule. Like many of us, you probably get up and feed the cat, make the coffee, take your shower, make breakfast, figure out what to wear that is semi-clean, and rush around to get yourself and everyone else in your household out of the door and off to where they need to go (hopefully on time).

In my household it usually means asking my daughter to hurry up and eat her breakfast about twenty times, hurry up and get dressed about ten times, and hurry up and use the bathroom and get her teeth brushed about five times. We have tears at our house three or four times before we even get out of the door most mornings. And yes, it could be her or me crying by the one hundredth time I have asked her to do what needs to be done the same way every single day.

After the morning chaos and drama, you probably walk or drive your kids to school, race as fast as you can to get to work, and start your work routine, which I imagine for many is just as hectic as your morning routine at home. We all know and experience this as our daily grind. It's all important and we all have to do it, but it is exhausting. Just writing this makes my shoulders rise up and almost touch my ears from stress. I want to stop and take a moment to catch my breath, and I wonder how we accomplish this every single day without losing our minds. As you think about your morning routine, just getting through it all day after day, how does it make you feel? Have you had a chance to enjoy anything so far today? Or are you just wishing for the weekend in hopes that you may get to do something you want to do and break out of the monotony? Let's get real for a minute. Dreaming about the weekend is just a fantasy, because the truth is, we just have different crazy routines on the weekends. All this is sounding a little familiar, isn't it?

Life Lesson #2 from my five-year-old: Pay attention to what is happening to you at this very moment.

"You can't change somebody else. You can only change yourself."

You get to choose what to focus on. That is about as basic as it gets. Experience the world from the perspective of a five-year-old, and it will transport you immediately back to the basics, maximizing all of your senses and focusing on what really is important.

Think about morning rituals again, in a slightly different way. I realize that much of the drama with my daughter in the mornings is caused by my stress in trying to get us ready and out the door on time. So, view this again but through the lens of a five-year-old. Use all of your senses, be in the moment, and see how the morning grind could look different and ultimately change the start and outcome of your entire day.

This time, after you get up in the morning, start by petting the cat for just a few minutes. Enjoy the smell of the coffee. As you fix breakfast, feel grateful that you have food to give your family. Appreciate the gift of your child, your spouse, your parent, even your pet. As you are walking or driving your kids to school, talk about whatever makes you happy. Talk about what is happening in school that day, or enjoy the sun or rain or snow that is coming down. Really connect and engage with them so that they start the day off feeling loved, appreciated, heard, and validated. Then you'll arrive at work ready to start your day.

Does this feel different than your normal approach, or is this already how you manage your everyday routines? If it's how you manage, good for you, because I imagine you are able to handle the challenges of the day and the flexibility required from a much more grounded place. Making a small shift in how you approach the ordinary tasks of your day will help you start your day from a much different place than that of just surviving the daily grind. It allows you to be more in touch with who you really are, what you really need, and what is most important to you.

I had a little get-together with some moms from my daughter's class one evening. We were chatting about lots of things, and I brought up this notion of really being present with your kids and how hard it is sometimes. It certainly isn't a new concept, but it is one that deserves attention every now and then. All of the moms that night were talking about how we do the best we can on a daily basis to be there for our kids, but it is a challenge given everything we have to juggle on a daily basis. It was a great conversation that helped to validate for each of us that we do know what is important and do the best we can every day. A few weeks later, I received an e-mail from one of the moms who had joined in this conversation. She told me that just having that conversation helped her be present for a very cute moment with her daughter. By really being present for her daughter in that moment, she realized how much she had been missing.

We all need support and a little reminder from time to time of what matters in our lives, and we shouldn't be hard on ourselves when we can't always be there physically or emotionally. The important thing is to maximize the time you are present and emotionally available for yourself, your kids, and your family. You will begin to see things differently, begin to get stronger, and begin to allow your true voice and purpose to come through. This can be the beginning of your heart and mind awakening to who you really are and the gifts you have to offer.

Life Lesson #2 from my five-year-old: Remember that you can't change other people, so focus on yourself.

Put It into Practice: Reconnect with your basic senses, and you will reconnect with who you are and what you care about.

- Make the effort, starting today, to do one of these things: use your sense of *smell*, really *hear* your favorite song, go to the flower mart or grocery store and *see* the miracle of a single flower, really *taste* the food you are eating, pet your cat and *feel* the softness of her fur or enjoy the warmth of the sun on your face.
- Pay attention to how you feel. Do you feel any different, interact with people any differently, and most important, quiet that negative voice in your head, allowing you to understand who you really are and what you have to offer the world and those around you? You will begin to feel more in balance and calmer immediately.

Take a couple of deep breaths and exhale the daily grind. It takes only a few minutes a day, and you will be able to clear your head and open your heart to even more possibilities just waiting to surface.

Notes

Notes

Chapter 3: We Have This Moment—Guaranteed

———◦⋄⁂⋄◦———

"If you're going to live your life, do it now!"
—B, Age 5

IT WAS OUR FIRST WINTER living in New York City, and the news was making a big deal about a major winter storm coming and how much snow it was going to drop. I said bring it on! This year there was no shoveling of the driveway or driving in the snow for us. I didn't have a care in the world and could hardly wait for the snow to start falling. My daughter and I waited all day, but it still hadn't started snowing when she had to go to bed. So I made her a promise. I promised that if it started snowing before I went to bed, I would wake her up so she could see the snow coming down.

At about nine thirty that night, I looked out the window to see the snow coming down hard. There was already a ton of snow on the ground.

I got excited and ran in to wake her up so she could come and look at the snow falling. When I woke her up, we both ran back to the window and together watched the snow falling for a while. Then I said, "Let's put on our hats and coats, boots and mittens, and go play in the snow for a little while." So we pulled on our gear right over our pajamas, and outside we went. It was so beautiful and the snow on the sidewalks was untouched. My daughter went running into the snow laughing and playing, and dropping every five feet on untouched snow to create one perfect snow angel after another. We took pictures and caught big fluffy snowflakes on our tongues. We must have been outside only fifteen minutes total and walked only about a block, but I have to tell you that to this day that is one of our favorite memories. It was one of those extraordinary moments that we will both always remember. Instead of doing the logical thing and staying inside where it was warm and dry, we embraced the moment and created a memory that will last a lifetime.

Another favorite memory is from when B's grandma was in town and staying with us for two weeks, which was such a special treat for us. We had decided to go out to dinner, a regular occurrence for us, and were getting ready to walk out the door when B came around the corner wearing quite the outfit. She had on a tiger visor, her backpack stuffed with who knows what, and held a whistle in her hand. I was not certain what she had in mind, but it didn't matter; we just decided to go with it. She could wear or take whatever she wanted to the restaurant. So we got down to the sidewalk and headed down the street to the restaurant. Our little leader began to blow this terrible, high-pitched whistle, making all of the dogs in the neighborhood go nuts, and then she started hollering at us to follow her, get in line, and begin marching. So off we all went in single file down the street behind our tiger-visor, Dora-backpack-wearing band leader, blowing her whistle and hollering "Hup two, three, four ... I can't hear you!" Needless to say, we quickly got in line at our fearless leader's direction. I'd had a really hard day at work that day and struggled to be fully present. In that moment, I recognized this as an amazing moment, and I had to force myself to switch gears, unload the unpleasant workday, and be present to appreciate the irreplaceable moment I was experiencing.

The truth is, sometimes it is hard to switch gears, and we have to make that conscious effort. I am so grateful that I recognized this extraordinary moment with my mom and daughter. It was just a silly little thing, but it still makes me smile as I remember the way we proudly marched down the street in single file.

How often do you find yourself either thinking or saying, "I will get to that tomorrow"? Or "I don't have time to think about that today because I have too much going on." The reality is, we all probably do have too much going on, and that is very much a part of each of our daily realities. What I am learning is that extraordinary things happen to each of us every single day if we are willing to open our eyes and see what is really going on around us. As I take time to think back over the last few years, I am able to recall some pretty amazing everyday occurrences that, fortunately, I was emotionally and physically present for.

Extraordinary things really do happen each and every day, and sometimes it means we just need to look at a situation through a different lens, as happened when we went to the grocery store one night. My daughter brought a puzzle with her that had all these bright colors in it, and she went around the grocery store looking for foods to match the colors. I have to be honest with you—I think I enjoyed it as much as she did, because I saw ordinary everyday fruits and vegetables in an entirely new light. It pulled me from the craziness of the day and landed me firmly in my own skin, in the right here and the right now, a pretty good place to be.

One evening during my daughter's bath time, she was playing and having a good old time in the tub when out of the blue she announced very emphatically, *"If you're going to live your life, do it now!"* It caught me completely off guard; it was such a random but profound proclamation. And then she turned right back to making more soap-bubble art on the side of the bathtub. My only response was that I completely agreed with her. I sat there at the side of the tub thinking about her comment for quite a while as she continued to get pruney fingers and toes from her soak. What are we really waiting for, and is there anything holding us back from living our lives right this very minute? The words *"do it now"* pretty much say it all, don't they? How do I *"do it now"* if I'm not 100 percent sure of what I'm not doing?

Life Lesson #3 from my five-year-old:
What exactly are you waiting for? Something in the
future that may or may not ever happen?

"If you're going to live your life, do it now!"

Let me tell you about an ordinary occurrence that turned out to be quite extraordinary and is a perfect example of living your life right now. A friend of mine sadly lost her father to an unfortunate disease, and before he passed, the family came together to enjoy every moment they had with him. Even while making sure there were no unsaid words, and that they had come to terms the best they could with the inevitable, they never lost their hope or faith.

They are an amazingly tight-knit family, which you can't help but admire. This family certainly forced themselves to be present in their own lives and appreciate every moment that they had together. I'm not saying they weren't close prior to this; I'm only sharing my observation that their awareness of the reality of this important life event increased their need and desire to appreciate every moment they had together.

Recently, my friend and I were talking, and she told me that after her dad passed, her mom gave her a special gift. Her dad had kept every card she had ever given him. She was shocked when she learned this, because she'd had no idea that he had. The simple greeting cards she had sent to her dad over the years had a much bigger impact than she had ever known.

This ordinary bunch of greeting cards made a big and lasting impact; it was an extraordinary gift that gave twofold. Sending the cards to her father gave him joy over the years, and finding out that he had saved every card she had given him gave my friend great comfort and validation of her father's love for her.

Don't wish your days and weeks away. Instead, choose to be right where you are, in the here and now, and not miss the extraordinary things and people that are in your life today. Let go of that thousand-pound weight on your shoulders, and free your mind to think about and explore something so much bigger and more powerful than what your everyday life may be delivering.

Life Lesson #3 from my five-year-old: Really live your life every day—starting right now!

Put It into Practice: Give yourself permission to enjoy and appreciate the extraordinary moments that happen in your life every day.

- Find a quiet place in your home or wherever you feel happiest or most comfortable. Take a couple of deep breaths, quiet your mind, and think back over the last week, month, or year for a couple of things that have happened to you or that you participated in that were truly extraordinary. They don't have to be major, life-altering events—just a couple of things you can remember that were important to you, such as going for a long run, starting a new class, or planning a big event like a wedding or anniversary.
- As you think about these events or moments, how do you feel physically? Does remembering make you smile? Do you feel any of the stress leaving your shoulders, or wherever you hold your stress, and do you feel lighter, more in balance and centered?
- What could you do for someone else at this very minute that you would think of as a normal occurrence, but which could be quite extraordinary for the recipient? A phone call to someone just to see how he or she is doing? A knock on your neighbor's door to take them something you know he or she would love or just to say hello? Your action could have a much bigger effect than you can even imagine.

It's time to make a difference not only for yourself but for others, beginning with this moment. Don't settle for just existing: live your life right now, and find the little things that truly make you happy.

Notes

Notes

Chapter 4: Happiness Is ...

"I love my life!"

—B, Age 5

Not long after we moved to New York City, we had one of those really nasty rainy days. It was raining hard and I still hadn't figured out all of the stroller gear, the umbrella situation, and the boots and coat needed to help us manage living in an urban environment when it rains.

I picked B up from day care, and we finally got to the subway station, dripping wet. We were both more than ready to head home. But the subway was absolutely packed, so I had to ask B to get out of her stroller, and I had to fold it up and carry it. We squeezed onto the subway, and I was holding the wet stroller and feeling the water drip down my arm. I was beyond miserable! Just then I looked down at B crammed in between all of the adults towering above her, and she was proudly holding on to the subway pole like a big kid. She looked up at me with a big smile on her face and said, "I love living here." To her, it was this big adventure. I definitely have a pretty amazing little girl who has this ability to put a positive spin on a situation that could otherwise be perceived as an unpleasant moment in an absolutely miserable day.

The truth is, she actually did, and still does, love living in New York City. She has become a true New Yorker in every sense of the word. In that moment, she felt like a big kid out of her stroller and standing in the crowded subway car with all of the adults. She loved the energy of New York and what our life had become. It took me by surprise since I was feeling the absolute opposite at that moment—tired, wet, dripped on, and squished, just wishing we were home. The smile on her face said it all to me. She had that look of complete and utter peace and happiness about her.

Happiness. Peace. Contentment. I don't know about you, but these are not concepts that I generally think of every day, let alone experience. I am just being honest. Very few people walk around without a care in the world every day and, if they do, don't you look at them with disbelief? I mean, get real. Most of us have a different reality. So how can we make happiness, peace, and contentment more of our daily reality? How can we create moments of peace or joy in our lives and draw upon those experiences to help us get through some of the less-than-pleasant ones?

When was the last time you felt sheer joy or happiness? I mean that honest-to-goodness "I am going to burst because I am so happy" feeling? When you stop to think about it, being happy—finding moments of peace or moments of pure contentment—doesn't have to be about big moments at all. You can start by appreciating the small things and work your way up to the really big "never want to forget this feeling" moments.

So where do you find it? Maybe it is pizza-and-movie night, or maybe finding five minutes to do absolutely nothing and enjoy a few moments of peace and quiet with a nice glass of wine. You see, I don't think any of us will ever find that peace and happiness every moment of every day, despite the Grimm brothers' valiant efforts, with their once-upon-a-times and happily-ever-afters. If only life were that easy.

But maybe it was, once, that easy for all of us. Children see life simply, but always truthfully. My daughter sees life differently than adults do. She hasn't had enough time to have "reality" heaped on her head on a daily basis, and her brain isn't overly saturated with the millions of things that must be done every single day. She still skips down the street to go to the local donut shop in sheer bliss, and she shouts out at the top of her lungs as she skips, "I love my life," just because she can. It's possible that you have greatly underestimated the power of skipping on your way to eat donuts. It should be high on the list of how to lift your spirits and make you smile. Maybe you should add that one to your bucket list!

Life Lesson #4 from my five-year-old:
If you aren't experiencing happiness or peace, what are you going to do about it? You too can experience those moments that make you want to shout out at the top of your lungs,

"I love my life!"

Not that many years ago, my nickname at work was Mary Sunshine, which kind of makes me chuckle now. I generally projected a very positive and bubbly image, but the truth was, I didn't always feel that way. At the time, it was the image I chose to project even though it wasn't how I necessarily always felt. Now that I am older, not really wiser, and don't really care when I come off a little surly at work, I sometimes think back to my Mary Sunshine days. Was life easier back then? The truth is yes, I think it was. I sometimes wish I could find that more carefree person, so that I could give myself permission to laugh a little more and not take myself so seriously. How can you find those moments of just loving your life? Are they always the same, or have they grown up and evolved with you over the years? What I have learned is how to face reality while appreciating both the small and the big moments along the way.

I readily acknowledge that some of my choices have made my life more challenging at times. It was my choice to become a single parent later in life. But for me this decision has brought some definite advantages. For good or for bad (or a little of both), my daughter goes without very little. We have been extremely fortunate to travel quite a bit and enjoy some very nice vacations with our family. When I told my daughter that when I was a kid my family went on only one vacation ever, she could not comprehend it, because she has already been to so many places in her short five years on this earth. On one of our family vacations, I had to take a few minutes to ground myself and remember what is really important. I am lucky that my family gave me an hour to myself so I could rejuvenate a little. It gave me a few minutes to take a deep breath, drink a good cup of coffee, clear out all of the cobwebs in my head, and appreciate the good things in my life. This little bit of time, just for me, was all I needed to find my piece of peace. The last night of our vacation, we all went around the table and shared either what we were thankful for or one of the highlights from the trip. When it got to my daughter, she said, "I am thankful I was adopted into this family." My heart opened up and exploded with a kind of joy and happiness that is indescribable. I had no words that could compare with the truth that had been revealed by my young daughter. All I could do was look at her and smile while tears streamed down my face. How was I worthy of this little girl? I don't know that answer but am grateful for the gift I have been given. That was a great moment, a tearjerker I-love-my-life moment to remember always; it left me completely speechless and profoundly grateful.

"I love my life" is such an interesting and big concept. Its challenge, of course, is found in the reality of your everyday life, not on vacation. How do you create those moments for yourself so that you remember how good you have it? How do you break it down so that it is attainable for you? Or what if there is nothing in your life that makes you happy or gives you a moment of peace? How do you go about making the changes you need to get back to what really is important to you?

Even when you know you need to make changes in your life, the status quo is somehow more comfortable and familiar. This can keep you from making the change you know you need to make. Think about that for a second. What if you know you need to make a change for yourself, but the life you are living now is comfortable or familiar, even if it is not good for you? Translation: I know that some of the things I am doing right now aren't good for me, but, hey, continuing on this path is easier than making a change or experiencing the unknown. Does that make any bells or whistles go off in your head? If so, sit up and take note. You may not be able to make the kind of change you want to today. But you can certainly begin to create a plan to get you where you want to go. Along the way, begin to be aware of the moments that move you closer to living a more fulfilling life.

You actually do deserve the happily-ever-after, even if it isn't a Grimm brothers' version, but maybe a little more closely aligned with skipping down the sidewalk on the way to the donut shop!

Life Lesson #4 from my five-year-old: Happiness is a state of mind, a feeling, an expression of moments you experience. Choose it!

Put It into Practice: What does your happily-ever-after moment look like? Small moments can be just as important as big, life-altering ones!

- You don't live in a fairy tale, so what does a realistic happily-ever-after, love-your-life moment look like? These moments can be small or big, such as making a healthier lunch choice or earning a degree.
- What can you do for yourself on a daily, weekly, or monthly basis that will allow you the time to unload some of the garbage and experience some of the good moments your life does offer? How can you make that happen for yourself?
- How does it make you feel when you think about making change in your life? Are you willing to move out of that familiar, comfortable place to make change happen for yourself? Start by setting two goals:

  * Make the first one a small, attainable goal, such as smiling at someone you don't know.
  * Make the second goal something that will help you stretch and grow.

What do you need to put in place to make these goals a reality? A great starting point is simply to begin to be thankful for what you have in your life at this very moment.

Notes

Notes

Chapter 5: It's about More Than Just Surviving

**"Oh, Mommy, don't let anyone control you
or stand in your way."**

—B, Age 5

My DAUGHTER WAS BORN IN a country where, in many cases, a young child is unable to attend school during the day, because she is working to help earn money so the family can eat. On one of my many visits to B's country before I was able to bring her home, I witnessed young children on street corners and in front of businesses, holding large machine guns. It was their job to protect the stores. The guns were literally half their size. Another vivid memory is of a seven- or eight-year-old girl selling jewelry in the streets during a time of the day that another group of children I witnessed were in school. The "working children" who were lucky enough to go to school at night have to share books with as many as ten other children just to have the opportunity to learn, something we sometimes take for granted here in the United States. I was and still am heartbroken to know what these children have to do just to pay for basic needs for themselves and for their families. It makes me grateful for and appreciative of the life I was and am able to live.

Many of us—myself included— have experienced times when we have lived paycheck to paycheck, sometimes without enough money left over to buy food. I remember those times vividly. I was working two jobs and still could barely make it, even then having to juggle paying the bills (or creative accounting, as I like to call it) to get everything to balance the best I could. It is a real situation for many people who live it every day, including people you know, friends and neighbors. What powers us forward or gives us the strength to keep putting one foot in front of the other when we feel like we are barely able to make it moment to moment? How do we continue to function in a day-to-day survival mode?

Your life must be about much more than just surviving. You may experience times in your life when the best you can do is just get through the week, day, or even hour. And when you feel like that, how can you focus on the things that really matter the most? I believe you must hope and *believe* that you deserve more in life, and then create opportunities to make your life richer.

Take an average American holiday season, for example; all you see on TV and in every form of media are amazing things we all wish we could have, but rarely need. And my daughter, just like many other children, wanted to visit Santa and tell him what she wished to receive for the holidays. We made our annual trip down to Macy's on Thirty-Fourth Street to the Santa Toyland and waited patiently in the seemingly never-ending line. When it was finally her turn to see Santa, she wasn't sure she could go through with it, but what happened instead was magical. Santa called her by name. He called her by name! He even said that he remembered visiting me, her dear old mom, when I was a little girl. He was so gentle and kind, and he made her feel like the special little girl that she is. After we took pictures with Santa and she had the chance to tell him that she wanted a coloring book for Christmas and a few other toys, we started to wander out of the store. She was enthralled with Santa, and she said to me that she thought he was very realistic-looking and that he might have actually been the real Santa, not just one of his helpers. I agreed that he was something special, for sure. She had that serene look that said "I believe in the magic of Santa Claus" written all over her face. She was full of hope and anticipation. Later that night, still basking in the afterglow of Santa Toyland, she surprised me by saying that the things that matter most can't be wrapped. I was proud of her for recognizing that material things are not what make us truly happy.

As I thought about it further after she went to sleep, I was trying to figure out how we can all move from that beaten-down state of mind of just surviving to more of an I-believe feeling full of hope and, dare I say, joyful place. Now I am not saying everyone should believe in Santa, of course. What I am saying is to look inside your heart and find what will nurture your soul. Find what will help you move from living in unfulfilling moments to experiencing moments that are awe-inspiring.

I would never make light of the situation of anyone truly doing their best to make sure that he or she or their family have their basic needs met. What I am asking is, How can we find a way to move ourselves forward from that place of lack or feeling of being unfulfilled to find a place that includes more abundance of spirit and happiness? As my daughter said to me one afternoon on our walk home from school when my spirit was running low, "Don't let anyone control you or stand in your way." To me, her statement was about determination and confidence. Her comment told me to take control and turn how I was feeling from just surviving to taking charge and thriving.

Life Lesson #5 from my five-year-old:
We are all much stronger than we know and have the capacity to change some situations from negative to positive by first making a shift in our attitude. Come from a place of perseverance and hope.

"Don't let anyone control you or stand in your way."

How many of us have said, "I just have to survive the week" or "I just have to get through this situation"? What does that make you think of, and how does it make you feel? If you are making this type of statement, you are probably not dealing with anything you even remotely *want* to deal with. I think that way too many of us are very familiar with living in an environment that sometimes makes us feel like "surviving vs. thriving." How do we move from barely getting by to appreciation, growth, and abundance? Well, that is a million-dollar question, and if you know a quick solution, you should package that and make your fortune! But the reality is that only we can make the shift happen for ourselves, and it isn't an all-or-nothing proposition.

I experienced a situation not long ago that left me feeling completely powerless and beyond frustrated. I had a property in another state that I had not been able to sell due to the economy, and so I had to rent it out for a few years. The individual who rented the property wasn't up front with me from the very beginning, which created tension and anxiety for me. On one hand, I was grateful to have someone paying rent and, on the other hand, felt completely out of control when it came to knowing the condition of what had been our home. I decided to put the property back on the market, which meant the renters were going to need to move out. Fortunately, they did. When I was able to get in and assess what needed to be done before I could put it on the market, I was devastated. What had been my home for so many years had been abused and lived in hard.

I kept thinking to myself that I just needed to survive the moment in order to get through it and manage all of the work I had to do. I felt exhausted from the stress of the situation. This negative situation zapped every bit of energy I had, and then, on top of it, I beat myself up for having fallen into emotionally charged interactions when dealing with the former renter. The reality is that we are human and we are not perfect—just in case you didn't realize that or needed to be reminded. I know that I am my harshest critic, and that no matter what anyone says to me or what I think he or she may say about me, it is never as bad as how I have already tortured myself. No one is harder on you than you. Wow, that stinks, doesn't it! But how we choose to deal with it is what is important.

So, as I thought back over that negative experience that was so hard, I felt like I could have managed it better from a human-behavior perspective and perhaps have been able to eliminate some of the stress I had to deal with. In stressful situations like this, I have started to measure myself on the length of time it takes me to pull out of this negative place. Does it take me two years, two months, two weeks, two days, or two minutes? How quickly I am able to let go of those negative thoughts and feelings is how I rate my progress. If I am able to move through my emotions more quickly than in the past, I am able to move through the emotions associated with the situation, instead of living in that perpetual mode of doom. I think the ultimate growth will be when I am able to not react emotionally to negativity at all, but hey, that gives me something to strive for!

Living in survival mode gets you through the day, but are you moving forward? Are you completing tasks and living life in the most productive way? In the particular situation I experienced, did we end up getting resolution on the situation? Yes. Did my response to this situation impact others in a negative way? Yes, a few. Could I have handled it differently? Oh, most definitely yes! I felt bad because I behaved in a way that I would never even dream of behaving. The bigger question to me was why. *Why* wasn't I able to rise above my frustration stemming from strong emotions happening all around me, to help come up with a rational solution that my former renter would be willing to listen and respond to? The answer is, sometimes you just have to survive the situation and do the best you can. Learn from it. Grow from it. Do your best not to repeat it.

My daughter and her cousin are polar opposites, the yin to the other's yang. They share a unique bond so special and strong, and together they balance out the other's extremes. Together they achieve balance. Maybe the starting point is to find another point of view that is opposite to yours, because the answer probably lies somewhere in between "just surviving" and "I believe." A perspective different from yours could help you see and create a new starting point or path.

Life Lesson #5 from my five-year-old: The truth is that we are human, and sometimes we do just have to survive. But rather than always just surviving, let's evolve. Find the yin to your yang that can give you a new perspective.

Put It into Practice: What makes you want to scream from the mountain tops, "*I believe!*"?

Think of a situation you have experienced recently, and look at it from the opposite viewpoint, to see what you can learn.

- Think of a situation that normally brings out your worst possible behavior and how you react. Now, what would happen if you thought about it from the completely opposite perspective? What do you think the outcome would be? Is there a middle ground you can reach and still have a better outcome than you would normally?

- What are you dealing with right now that puts you in the "just survive" mode? Can you think of one or two options that could be helpful to relieve some of your stress? Are you contributing to this stress by standing in your own way?

- What does your "I believe" state look like? Can you make a difference for yourself emotionally, physically, or spiritually? What steps can you take to bring you closer to that goal?

Look for the obstacles that can be removed to help move you forward toward your goal instead of remaining stagnant. Keep the energy moving in a positive way.

Notes

Notes

Chapter 6: There's Always Time for a Good Laugh

"Oh, that's a big butt!"

—B, Age 5

THERE ISN'T ANYTHING BETTER THAN a good old belly laugh, is there? I mean the kind of laugh from deep down inside that shakes you to your very core. Laughing is one of the greatest gifts ever, and I would rather be around people who make me laugh pretty much more than anything else in the world. You can't feel awful when you are laughing. It just isn't physically possible. I am a huge believer in comic relief and have absolutely no problem making fun of myself for a good laugh. I hope that you will find yourself laughing or crying tears of joy when you think back to some of the funniest experiences you can remember.

Why is it that some of the funniest stories somehow involve the bathroom, especially when kids are involved? They could involve bathroom words, things that happen in the bathroom, or things you hear kids say in public restrooms. You know what I am talking about. Kids will say whatever they see and think, much to their parents' dismay, especially when in public. One of my all-time favorite stories happened a few years ago, and to this day, every time I think about it, tears fill my eyes. I just can't help but laugh out loud and smile until my cheeks hurt.

I am about to share with you one of my most embarrassing but hilarious bathroom stories. My daughter and I were at our favorite diner one night, going through our usual routine. We sat down and said hello to all of the wait staff, as we continue to be regulars at a number of our favorite local restaurants. We ordered our food and then headed to the restroom to take care of business and wash our hands before our dinner arrived. Fortunately, the larger bathroom stall was available, which gave us more room with two people. My daughter, of course, took care of her business first, and then I thought, *Oh, since we're here, I might as well too*. Instead of standing in front of me, somehow B got to the side of the toilet and back toward the wall. As I was getting ready to sit down on the toilet, I heard these words come out of her mouth, very loudly: "Oh, that's a *big* butt!" Now, she didn't say it in a nasty way, but really as more of a matter-of-fact reporting to the rest of the people in the bathroom what she had just witnessed. I didn't know how to react; I didn't want her to think it was okay to say things like that, but my whole body was shaking as I sat on the toilet, trying to keep from laughing out loud. Of course, as soon as we finished up in the restroom, washed our hands, and headed back to our table, I called everyone I knew and told them the story. I laughed until my sides hurt. To this day, all I have to do to make myself laugh is to think of those five little words, "Oh, that's a *big* butt," and all is right in my world again.

Life Lesson #6 from my five-year-old:
There is nothing in the world like a good old-fashioned
belly laugh to put things into perspective.

"Oh, that's a big butt!"

Why am I willing to share this less-than-flattering anecdote? Well, because it just shows that we are all human. We have flaws and that is okay. And if we can find a way to laugh and lighten up a little bit, isn't life much more fun?

Not that long ago everyone knew me as the silly person at work and at home. I was constantly making others laugh and providing a little office comic relief and, quite honestly, cracking myself up as well. So what changed? Every now and then I tap back into that carefree spirit and feel about a hundred pounds lighter. What if we could continue to be our responsible selves while enjoying whatever it is we do just a little more, and laughing a whole lot more? I say, sign me up! It is so much easier to stay in that "unfun" but comfortable place; but it is so much more rewarding to seek out situations that allow you to feel more carefree, to let your hair down, act a little immature if you want to, and laugh until you cry.

Of course, we all have to be responsible for our actions; so be responsible for your actions, but find ways to loosen up too. Easier said than done, you might say, or Where do I start? How about recording your favorite show or movie that makes you laugh out loud and then watching it over and over again? Ridiculous? Absolutely! Fun? I think yes!

My niece, now age four, still runs in a more childlike way, and it is hilarious! One day when I was with her, I decided to just throw caution to the wind and started running like her. It not only made me laugh but made me not feel so serious for a few minutes. It was beyond ridiculous, and just what I needed to pull me out of my funk and focus on just feeling like a kid again. Don't be afraid to jump out of your comfort zone every now and then and be outrageous. You'll be surprised at just how liberating it can be!

One of my best friends for more than twenty-five years has to be one of the most ridiculous people I have ever known, and someone I can always count on for a good laugh. We have been friends since college, and she knows all of my stories and is more than willing to share with my daughter (which I know I will pay for one day). She has led a very colorful life that one day will be a best seller, when she finally puts all of her life experiences down on paper. It doesn't matter how much time goes by between our visits, because we always seem to pick up right where we left off. When we get together our combined maturity level can't be more than about twenty-five years old and usually involves a good bottle of wine followed by hours of laughter.

We are big into dancing in our household. Whenever B's favorite theme songs come on the TV, she has to jump off the couch and begin to dance. She will holler at me if I am in another room that "her groove" is on, just so I will come in and watch her dance. She has quite the moves! Every now and then I will make her laugh by jumping up with her, and we will have an impromptu dance party for about thirty seconds. Try to do that and not smile—it simply can't be done! Let yourself go a little, and when you hear "your groove" on the radio or in whatever store you are in, just start dancing, even a bit. I promise it will make you smile.

Just thinking about many of the truly ridiculous things I have done over my lifetime, down to even just the silliness of every day, makes me smile. But my true life mission is to constantly search for the next, "Oh, that's a *big* butt" life event, full of smile-induced cheek hurting and side-splitting belly laughing!

Life Lesson #6 from my five-year-old: Make sure you laugh a lot along the way; sometimes it's okay to just tell it like you see it.

Put It into Practice: What is your "Oh, that's a *big* butt" story? Everyone has one and if you don't, it's time to get one!

- Think back to a couple of times when you felt carefree and happy. What comes to mind? Do you remember what was happening in your life at that time?
- Now think about the last time you had a good old belly laugh. Was it recent? What was the situation? How did it make you feel? Using descriptive words, write it down.
- Think about three actions you can take to create moments or situations where you can let your hair down and have a good laugh; then make them happen.

I'm convinced that "a good laugh every day will help keep sadness away." What do you have to lose?!

Notes

Notes

Chapter 7: Are You Fearless or Fearful?

**"I'm so proud of myself. I did it!
This is the day I have been waiting for!"**

—B, Age 5

THE AMERICAN PASTOR AND AUTHOR Dr. Robert Schuller asked this powerful question: "What would you attempt to do if you knew you could not fail?" Without really thinking about it or letting your rational mind answer that question, what is your answer?

What a powerful thought, the notion of doing whatever you love and care about and not failing. I know when I first read that quote, so many thoughts and ideas came rushing to me, as did a sense of relief from some kind of pressure that I feel on a daily basis. For some time now I have been contemplating this question and others, trying to determine why I haven't been able to move my career and life forward. One of the answers that keeps surfacing for me is *fear*. But fear of what? Is it fear of failure or, crazier yet, fear of success? That doesn't even make sense to me. I understand being afraid to fail, but remind me again why. What's the worst thing that could happen if you actually failed at something?

And by the way, how many times have you really failed at anything you actually cared about? I pride myself on the notion that I simply do not fail. Now, I know that is somewhat arrogant of me, because we all fail at things sometimes, but it is indeed my mind-set. For me, failure has never been an option, at least when it comes to having and keeping a good job and ensuring that all of my basic needs and those of my daughter are met. In our case, our needs are more than met, yet I still find myself feeling moments of sheer panic whenever my livelihood feels the least bit threatened. Now, please note that I didn't say I really have had cause for concern about losing my means to pay my bills; rather, I'm talking about a perceived threat, real or imagined. In these economic times, there are plenty of reasons to feel justifiably threatened, and I am certainly not alone in that feeling.

This notion of recognizing what causes us to respond from a place of fear and that we have the power within ourselves to overcome it surfaced for me when I was struggling to find a way to help my daughter. I watched her struggling with a fear of putting her face in the water at swimming lessons. From my perspective, the fear was completely irrational, but to her it was very real. It upset me to witness her struggles, especially when I knew her fears weren't logical. For years, no matter how hard she tried during swimming lessons, she couldn't get past her fear of simply putting her face in the water. When I would ask her what she was afraid of, she wasn't able to articulate why it scared her, but she was able to express her frustration, mainly through tears. I knew all along that she could do it and that there was nothing to be afraid of, but I also knew that she had to work this out for herself. My job as her parent was to continue to reassure and encourage her to continue to do her best and be proud of what she was accomplishing, but I still felt helpless seeing her struggle.

So what did we do? We practiced over and over again in the bathtub, where she felt safe. Then one night, during the Sunday-night bath ritual, she was finally able to hold her breath and put her face all the way into the water by herself. We both screamed from excitement at this monumental accomplishment. The more she practiced in a safe environment, the more confident she became of being able to overcome her fear. You could see that she was freed from the fear that had kept her from moving forward. A few weeks later we went out of town and stayed at a hotel with a swimming pool, so we were able to work hard on her swimming. In the span of just a few short weeks, she moved from a place of being afraid to being able to swim halfway across the pool. I will never forget lifting her up high out of the water, hugging her, and telling her how proud I was of her; she said, "I'm so proud of myself. I did it. This is the day I have been waiting for!" She was so full of pride and through her courage was able to move from a paralyzed state to one of freedom, right before my eyes.

From my perspective, my daughter's fears should have been easy to overcome, and yet for her they were enormous. What she didn't do was give up. Instead, she acknowledged what she was afraid of and then drew upon her courage to move her through this moment of fear.

Life Lesson #7 from my five-year-old:
You already have the strength and courage inside of you to overcome your fears and achieve way more than you believe is possible. Today can be your day if you choose.

"I'm so proud of myself. I did it.
This is the day I have been waiting for!"

Fear is a complicated emotion, not necessarily grounded in logic. What makes some people fearless and able to achieve what they know they deserve? And what makes others have trouble understanding why they have not been able to achieve what they think they want or deserve? I think the answer is courage and perseverance that powers us through our fears.

I have finally been able to admit out loud that I have been my own worst enemy, and the only one who is getting in between me and my larger dream is me. So what is my larger dream? It is to have no regrets and to become the person I know I am down deep inside. I continue to be a work in progress, as we all are. When you experience moments of truly being all that you can be, it is like you become luminous, as though a bright floodlight has been turned on inside of you, for everyone to see. The truth is that we are all learning as we go, and it's through our day-to-day moments that we evolve into who we really are and stretch to who we can become.

For years now, those little negative voices in my head have done a number on me. In spite of the negative dialogue trying to influence me, I have still become successful personally and professionally, at least based on my definition of success. I can say with certainty that the life I am living right now is ten times more than I could have ever imagined for myself. From growing up on a farm in Kansas, to living in the Upper West Side of Manhattan, to my career success, to fulfilling my dream of being a parent, these accomplishments have far exceeded any expectations I had for myself. Part of me—the illogical part—says, "You have already achieved more than you ever even dared to dream, so what makes you think you still deserve more?" The part of me that knows my true capability is screaming back right now and trying to win this fight, saying, "Because I want more—and I actually deserve to dream big and make those dreams a reality."

I have an uncle who reached a huge level of success professionally as the chairman and CEO of one of the country's largest engineering firms. Growing up, I knew he had a really big job but had no idea what that meant; I certainly couldn't relate to the level of success he had achieved. To me, he was my uncle who worked really hard at his job during the week and worked in the yard on the weekends. What I have now realized is that yes, he was successful in his career, but he was also successful in his life. My aunt ran the household and managed all of the social events required for his position, which was a huge job. She also helped to ensure that he was engaged in his life with his three sons and, eventually, all of the grandkids. After retirement he continues to enjoy an amazing life, rich with family and friends and traveling the world. What I have learned from observing how he has chosen to live is that there is not just one way to define success; you must look at your life in its entirety.

So the question to me is whether we are more successful when we are powered by fear or by fearlessness. Let me share with you several moments when I have felt both fearless and fearful, and how I used courage to move forward.

My family is very musical. I have always been drawn to the arts and loved to perform. I can't explain why, but a stage is a comfortable place that gives me that feeling of coming home. It's as though a switch goes on inside of me, and I instantly feel alive and know exactly what to do. It is exciting and thrilling; the way it makes me feel alive is difficult to describe. It has never been about the applause, but more about the connection with the audience. I've always felt fearless on stage. Now that doesn't mean I wouldn't get nervous or even scared sometimes, but that has never stopped me. I was always able to draw upon my courage to push me forward, performing for an audience ranging in size from seventy to seven thousand. I have felt the connection with the audience in a way that says, "Here is my gift to you—take it, enjoy it, feel it, deserve it." In those moments I have felt 100 percent deserving of being exactly where I am at that moment in time. It's a magical feeling and the most powerful I have ever experienced. What I didn't know when I was performing that I understand now is that I have felt so alive and so comfortable in that environment because helping people feel or reconnect to themselves is closer to my being on the right path.

I had been in New York City for only about six weeks, working at a new job that I didn't have a clue about, when I found out I was going to have to get up in front of the entire company and speak. It was a full company meeting for which they had rented the ballroom at the Waldorf Astoria. I was going to have to get up on the stage in front of hundreds of people I now worked with to talk about this new job that I didn't understand. I thought I was going to be literally sick. How was I going to talk about this new job when my new boss and I were still trying to define our roles? The morning came. The ballroom was full and it was our turn to deliver our slides. My new boss went first and I stood off to the side of the podium, trying not to pass out. Then it was my turn.

I will never forget what happened next, as it was so remarkable. It was as if that switch went on and something inside of me took over. I felt myself stand a little taller, exude confidence, and engage with the audience to deliver the message in a meaningful way. It was a powerful moment for me, as I had been completely fearful of what I was going to say and how I would deliver the information. When the moment came I more than rose to the occasion; I soared. You see, it was never about how good a singer, performer, or presenter I was. It was really about something much bigger, something I wasn't able to fully understand until now. It was about being fully present and understanding that I'm at my best when I am engaged in something I'm passionate about. When I'm living the truth of who I really am, I know it down to my very core, and it is as if all of the stars line up and allow me to shine in a way I didn't know was possible.

When I have been on the path taking me in the wrong direction, the fear has been the strongest, as if to say "You are going the wrong way down a one-way street." Stop now and "recalculate your route." I have had glimpses of what makes me feel fearless about being on the right path and am now working toward fulfilling and living up to it. Please realize that by sharing this with you I am not saying "shoulda, woulda, coulda"; instead, I am saying I get it. I now understand. And sometimes we need the time to go through all the life experiences we do in order to be ready to live more fearlessly and trust what we know to be true. I have been able to pull from some kind of inner knowing that actually has always been there but "marinating" for many years until I was able to open my heart and mind to the truth that has been there all along.

We can use our fear to test our direction. A healthy fear is a natural defense mechanism that keeps us out of trouble. Just don't let fear paralyze you into doing nothing.

Life Lesson #7 from my five-year-old: We all go through times where we come from a place of fear, but it is how we choose to move through the fear that defines who we really are and who we choose to be.

Put It into Practice: What do you choose?

This is a challenging topic for many of us, so really take your time working through this exercise.

- List three times you reacted from a place of fear. Can you remember the details of what caused you to react the way you did? Write down as many of the details as you can remember. What was the incident? How did you initially respond? How did it make you feel, and how long did the feeling of fear stay with you? Did you have any physical reaction? How did you eventually work through the fear?

- Now write down at least one or two specific incidents where you were able to use your courage to push you forward. What was the incident and how did you respond? Did this response feel different from the others you wrote down previously; if so, how? What was the key difference?

- What can you change in your life to come from a place of living intentionally? Do you need to make different choices? Do you need to manage situations differently?

Fear can be a very powerful emotion, creating extremes from motivation to paralysis. Call upon your courage to help power you forward in understanding your fear or in creating necessary change.

Notes

Notes

Chapter 8: What's Your Value?

"If we were rich, we could buy everything our hearts deserve!"

—B, Age 5

VALUE. WHAT A COMPLICATED WORD. What do you value? What makes you feel valued? *Value* has many meanings: worth, importance, significance, respect. What kind of value do you attach to yourself? Do you appreciate yourself? Are you living a life that you feel you deserve, or are you constantly thinking about what you wish you could have? I would be interested in knowing exactly what is running through your mind right now, but I venture to guess that many of these words make you very uncomfortable. I don't know why it is, but many of us feel apologetic if something good happens to us. For some reason, we just don't think we deserve it. Why is that?

How many times each day do you apologize for something that you probably had nothing to do with? Be honest. I am guessing that you do multiple times before you have even made it to work or had your first cup of coffee. I am painfully aware of this with myself and trying to recognize when I say I'm sorry, why I am saying it and how often. It is a behavior that conjures feelings of inadequacy. I am usually the first person to apologize for something, even if it doesn't have anything to do with me. Why is that? I do not want this for myself, and I certainly do not want to pass this on to my young daughter. When and why does the shift take place from being willing to speak your mind to feeling apologetic for your every move?

An event that my daughter and I experienced one day on the subway allowed me to put into perspective my behavior. We were pushing through the crowd to exit when a woman bumped into us. I told my daughter to say "I'm sorry," and her response was "Why should I say sorry to her, when I was in front of her and she bumped into me?" I had to think about it for a few minutes. Part of me wanted to say because when people are rude to us we need to be polite, but then I stopped myself because I realized my five-year-old was right. The woman who bumped into her should have excused herself, not the other way around. My daughter understood her self-worth better than I did, and it took me by surprise. I completely backed off my request for her to apologize to the woman, because she was so adamant that she didn't do anything wrong that she continued to argue with me all the way out of the subway station. She was looking to me for an answer as to why in the world I asked her to apologize, and the truth was that I didn't have one. She was right. For my daughter, it wasn't about entitlement. It was about respecting her space and her own worth.

That was a powerful moment for me. I didn't want to push onto my daughter my learned behavior of always assuming the responsibility of being wrong. I don't want her to ever think that her space, her being, her feelings about herself should take a back seat to anyone else. I don't want to raise a rude child, but on the other hand, I don't want to squelch her confidence or teach her to assume responsibility for other people's bad behavior.

I sometimes wish I could go back in time to when I had no inhibitions, no feeling of wanting to fit in socially. My daughter got these cute animal masks for the holidays one year. She particularly loved the tiger mask. I had to take her into work with me one day over her winter break, and I knew it wouldn't be a problem because many people would still be on holiday. She packed up her backpack, and off we went to my office, which was always a special treat for her. We finished up work and were putting on our coats to head home. She got her coat, hat, and backpack on, and I turned around to see she also had on her tiger mask. I thought, *Oh, well, doesn't bother me if it doesn't bother you.* I figured she would leave it on for about five minutes and then get bored with it. Oh boy, was I wrong! She left the mask on as we paraded through my office saying good-bye to my coworkers, down the elevator, out onto the street, and onto the subway. She sat there proudly wearing her tiger mask all the way home. Everyone around us couldn't help but smile when they saw her, because it was so unexpected and she looked so cute. I loved and admired her for not caring about anything other than doing her own thing. She knew people were looking at her, and she could not have cared less.

Most of my life I have tried to overcome my inability to appreciate my own value. I am interested in figuring out how to just be okay with who I am at this moment, and I continue to work on it daily. What do you believe your worth is? What is it that we actually deserve? I find it fascinating even in the work environment to look around the table at big meetings and wonder how some individuals have been able to catapult into senior-level positions, while others are doing their best to be invisible. Self-worth … entitlement … success … confidence: all interesting and powerful concepts that have different meanings and interpretations for each person.

Life Lesson #8 from my five-year-old:
You must realize that you deserve good things in your life
and that you are the one who has to believe it.

"If we were rich, we could buy everything
our hearts deserve."

I wonder to what extent our beliefs and inner strength are part of who we are when we come into this world, and how much is shaped by the environment. There are a number of famous people who have talked about coming from a background of abuse and extreme poverty and pulling themselves out of it to create amazing lives for themselves. Was that sheer determination that drove them forward? I don't know the answer, but I can tell you that it is extremely inspiring for all of us.

It's important that we don't downplay who we are and what we deserve in life. The truth is that each of us deserves so much more than what we will ever recognize for ourselves, and I am not talking about just material items.

What about work? Do you deserve a promotion you haven't gotten yet? Have you made it known to key leaders who can help you achieve your goals? Does your job or title define your value? I have worked with too many people who defined their value based on the title of their job. Someone sat in my office one day and told me that her job was all that she had and that being promoted was the only thing she cared about. This employee had more going for her than most, and yet her self-esteem and self-worth were based on a job title. Isn't it more important to enjoy your job and value yourself based on who you are as a person and what your larger contribution to the world is? I'm not downplaying the importance of upward mobility in your career. The larger and more important point is that I hope that any one thing in your life isn't your everything. There are many facets to our lives that help to shape who we are. They include not only our personal and professional accomplishments but equally who we are mentally, physically, and spiritually.

What about relationships? Do you deserve to have a happy relationship? The answer is simple: yes, of course you do. We all do. I'm still hoping my Mr. Wonderful shows up one day, and sooner rather than later. Everyone deserves to have the things in life that are important to them. However, nothing in life is ever perfect. The larger point is that we are all human beings who deserve to be treated in a way that is respectful and full of love. It is your responsibility to first make sure that you know what it is you want and deserve.

Every now and then I need to be reminded of how fortunate I truly am. When I tell my story to others, I am sometimes shocked when I realize how extraordinary my life really is. It forces me to reflect on and appreciate the success I have achieved in all areas of my life. The truth is I am grateful that I didn't marry any of the men I have dated so far. I look back now and count my blessings for having survived some probable train wrecks in that area. Remarkably I still believe in love and know that the right person will surface when we both have gone through the life experiences necessary to prepare us for a love and commitment for which we are both ready. I am beyond grateful that I had the courage to fulfill my dream of being a parent, and even more so since I accomplished this in a less-than-traditional way. I am grateful that I have always had good jobs and a career that continues to grow. I am also grateful that I am about 90–95 percent there when it comes to believing that I deserve all of this and more.

It is a constant journey but you must believe in yourself and know what you deserve in order to achieve what you want most in your life. You *do* deserve this or something better. Now it's time for you to believe it and go get it.

Life Lesson #8 from my five-year-old: It's not really just about what we want in life; it is what we believe we deserve.

Put It into Practice: It's okay to say out loud what your value is, and then you must believe it. What you deserve in life is up to you.

- Write down what it is you believe you deserve. It could be material things, or how you feel, or what you want in your life, such as a new job, a different car, or just to be happy. Do you know what you want? If not, that is definitely the starting point. What you want is probably a lot more basic than you imagine, so use that as your starting point and come up with three things you really want more in or from your life.
- How many of the things on your list do you have or are you in the process of getting or achieving?
- What can you do to help move this forward—what's your plan? Here are some initial thought starters to help you move forward in creating your plan to meet your goal.

  * What do you want to accomplish?
  * Who or what can help you accomplish your goal?

      *   What is your time frame? Be sure to include short-term and long-term milestones to help motivate you to keep moving forward.

Acknowledging what you want out loud is a major first step. Creating a plan will help you put the steps in place to help you move closer to reaching your goals.

Notes

Notes

_____

_____

_____

_____

_____

_____

_____

_____

_____

_____

_____

_____

_____

_____

_____

_____

_____

_____

_____

Chapter 9: Moments of Clarity

―⦿⦿⦿―

"I don't know how I know. I just know it."

—B, Age 5

SOME PEOPLE ARE VERY IN tune with their intuition. I met someone not so long ago who had been around my daughter for only about twenty minutes when she commented to me, "it is as if she is not of this world." My daughter came into this world with a strong sense of what she is to accomplish during her lifetime. She is my little angel and carries the weight of her instinctual blessing and burden. She is very proud of her heritage and has a huge desire to help the people from her country. My daughter also has a sense of connectedness with a power greater than any of us.

She has made statements about the fact that God is all around us all of the time and that he is our teacher and we are his children. This is significant because we have not been regular churchgoers, and yet she instinctively seems to have a direct ethereal connection to the higher power. The other day she was telling me about the angels. She went into great detail about what they say to her, what their wings look like and are made from. She says that she sees the angels at school sometimes and that they hang out in the classroom to give the students encouragement. She said there were five of them in the gym the other day, cheering the kids on. Ironically, gym is one of the things at school that gives my daughter a bit of a challenge because it is not her strong suit. I don't doubt a bit that this was one of the places she saw the angels offering encouragement and support.

I am constantly amazed by some of the comments she makes with the utmost certainty. When I ask her how she knows, her response, accompanied by a shrug of her shoulders, is, "I don't know how I know. I just know it." How many times have you just known and either acknowledged or disregarded these thoughts when you know them to be true?

There are times when I experience moments of absolute clarity. In those times, I am able to be decisive and take action even when there is a big and life-altering decision involved. Sometimes you just know in your gut and your heart what the answer is. It is in those moments of clarity that you know and trust that you are making the right decision because there is a force bigger than you carrying and guiding you down the right path.

I can easily recall a few distinct moments of absolute clarity. When I first moved to New York City, I had a terrible job in a very challenging environment. After only about six months, I knew this job just wasn't working for me, no matter how hard I tried. I needed to make a change. Going back to Kansas City wasn't the answer, so I needed to figure out how to find new opportunities in New York, and fast. One night I was walking out of work onto Forty-Second Street across from Bryant Park at about eight or nine p.m. I remember very clearly how I felt and what I thought. I looked at the city bus pulling up, and I thought that it would be less painful to be hit by that bus than to continue working at my job. It shook me to my core, because I am not someone who ever has thoughts like that, and the message could not have been any louder or more direct: "Attention! Attention! You are on the wrong path!" Talk about a moment of clarity! The message was to make a change, and make it right now.

Fortunately, I had been looking for a new job and was able to close the deal within about two weeks and move on. Once I had absolute clarity on what I needed to do, I was able to make it happen.

Another extreme moment of clarity came only a few years ago. The company I was working for moved the office I was working in to New York City. I was commuting about five hours a day, was a single parent, and both my stress level and my daughter's were through the roof. It was not a manageable situation for either of us. We had been trying to sell our condo for about a year and had had no luck. I kept thinking that when our condo sold, then we could move into New York City and make our lives much easier. One day after work and before I started my commute home, I stopped at one of the day care centers I was considering for my daughter. I walked out of the building where the day care was located, and my head was spinning because I knew it was not an option for us and that I needed to figure out another option quickly. I had no idea what I was going to do. It was an overwhelming feeling, knowing that we needed to make the move into the city and that day care was the first thing I needed to secure.

As I walked down the street searching for an answer, I remembered that a friend of mine had recommended that I check out a day care she had researched and really liked. I had visited the center and put our names on the waiting list about six months before but had not been in contact with them since. Would you believe that when I called them, they not only still had our names on the list but had availability beginning in less than a month? I took it without doubt and began the process of figuring out how to arrange the rest of our lives, including finding the right school district to move into, renting an apartment in the school district I chose, and then figuring out what to do with our condo. Within a week, I decided to change the listing on the condo from purchase to rental and was able to rent it out two weeks later. I knew, without question, what I needed to do, so I moved into action, and everything fell into place. It was still a very stressful time, but I had no doubt that I was making the right choices for my family. I just believed and trusted, knowing beyond a shadow of a doubt that I was making all of the right moves.

The truth is, sometimes there is no logical answer about how you know whether you are making the right decision. Sometimes you need to trust that sense of knowing or gut feeling and move forward with faith and confidence, knowing that if you need to correct or modify your course later on, that it's okay.

Life Lesson #9 from my five-year-old:
Trust your moments of clarity and the knowing we all have
deep inside. Sometimes there is no rational answer.

"I don't know how I know. I just know it."

A friend of mine was a single parent to an adopted little boy. She decided she was going to go through the arduous process again and adopt a second child. She was very clear about what she wanted, which was to adopt another child from the same country as her son, using the same adoption agency she had used before. Everything was going slowly but smoothly, and then she got a call that completely took her by surprise. Her son's biological cousin had been put up for adoption—a baby girl. It was as if in an instant that decision was made for her, not by her. I believe it was a force much larger than us that had a hand in this and put these two biological relatives together. Once she was able to get over the shock, excitement, and the sheer terror of adopting an infant that hadn't been part of *her* plan, she experienced a moment of clarity and a sense of knowing that while she had a choice adopting this little girl, this was absolutely the right decision. Really though, this decision had been made for her, not by her ... and it was a big one!

If the path you are on seems like a constant uphill battle and harder than it really needs to be, chances are you may want to stop and evaluate. You have a purpose or a path, and the doors open when you step in the right direction. Now, that is not to say that it won't be without work or that negative forces won't try to dissuade you. But when you are moving in the right direction, you know it—you feel it. Listen to your gut and your sense of knowing and trust it.

Life Lesson #9 from my five-year-old: Sometimes we don't need to question how we know the answers. The right path will reveal itself if you are willing to see it. Then it is up to you to jump the curb and roadblocks and go with the flow, not against it.

Put It into Practice: Trust yourself because you know a whole lot more than you give yourself credit for.

- Think back on some of the decisions you have made where you just knew beyond a shadow of a doubt that you were making the right one, a time when you trusted your gut. Did it have a positive outcome?
- Now think of a time when you weighed all of your options in a logical, well-thought-out approach based on facts. How did that situation turn out for you?
- Finally, think of a situation where your gut was telling you one thing and your logical approach told you something different. Which outcome do you believe in this situation would have been the better outcome: following your gut or making a logical, fact-based decision, or maybe a combination of the two?

Be aware of moments of clarity you receive that help guide you down your path. You always have the option to course-correct if necessary, but you must keep moving forward.

Notes

Notes

Chapter 10: This Is It

———∘◦⊱✿⊰◦∘———

"We all have our own path to follow."

—B, Age 5

THE JOURNEY I HAVE BEEN on and am sharing with you is really about the message of being true to who you are at your very core and making sure you live your life in the here and now. What is the one thing that makes you feel so passionate that every hair follicle tingles at the mere thought of doing it? It doesn't have to make you money or be a full-time profession, but it could be your hidden passion that you have suppressed for whatever reason. Now is the time to let your five-, fifteen-, or twenty-five-year-old self awaken again to the possibilities and the pure enjoyment, laughter, and happiness your heart *deserves*.

As you may have gathered by now, my five-year-old is unique and special in her own way, and I love her very much. I also like to tease her quite a bit, because some of the thoughts and comments she has are so beyond her years. She is like a wise ninety-five-year-old, whom I have fondly nicknamed "Estelle," who has had lifetimes chock-full of experiences. I half expect to hear words like *galoshes* and phrases like "back in the day when I was a kid" come out of her mouth.

What I know for sure is that adopting this little girl was the best thing I have ever done in my life. As my daughter has said, "We all have our own path to follow," and she is absolutely correct. No one can or should decide that for you. If you are on the wrong path, chances are no one needs to tell you, because you already know it. What is important is what you choose to do with that realization.

I think it is important to openly acknowledge that if I had chosen to do nothing differently, my life as it had been before I started this journey of self-exploration through writing this book would have been more than just fine—extraordinary, actually. For me, I just knew that there was something more in life that I needed to pursue for myself, and ultimately for my daughter. And that is to take the gifts I have been given and consciously make a difference in this world, whether with one person at a time or thousands. I choose to be a positive influence and role model for my daughter, to help her understand and own who she is and have the courage to live out what her dreams become.

I feel very fortunate to have accomplished what I have so far in this life, and I'm now even more interested and excited to see where this path will lead. When I need to adjust if I lean too far one way or another, I now know that I can and that nothing can stop me. You too have your own path to follow, and I hope you are on your way.

Life Lesson #10 from my five-year-old: Understand who you really are and what your very unique and special gift is to this world, and then find a way to live it.

Put It into Practice: Connect your extraordinary moments and create your path filled with peace, joy, and success!

1. **To Risk or Not to Risk, That Was My Question:** All of the risks and emotional hurdles can help move you from the off ramp back

onto the main road moving forward. Trust yourself—you already know the answers.

2. **Back to the Basics:** Remember that you can't change other people, so focus on yourself. Reconnect with your basic senses, and you will reconnect with who you are and what you care about.

3. **We Have This Moment—Guaranteed:** Really live your life every day—starting right now! Give yourself permission to enjoy and appreciate the extraordinary moments that happen in your life every day.

4. **Happiness Is …:** Happiness is a state of mind, a feeling, an expression of moments you experience. Choose it! What does your happily-ever-after moment look like? Small moments can be just as important as big, life-altering ones!

5. **It's about More Than Just Surviving:** The truth is that we are human, and sometimes we do have to just survive. But rather than always just surviving, let's evolve. Find the yin to your yang that can give you a new perspective. What makes you want to scream from the mountaintops, "*I believe!*"?

6. **There's Always Time for a Good Laugh:** Make sure you laugh a lot along the way; sometimes it's okay to just tell it like you see it. What is your "Oh, that's a *big* butt" story? Everyone has one and if you don't, it's time to get one!

7. **Are You Fearless or Fearful?:** We all go through times when we come from a place of fear, but it is how we choose to move through the fear that defines who we really are and who we choose to be. What do you choose?

8. **What's Your Value?** It's not really just about what we want in life; it is what we believe we deserve. It's okay to say out loud what your value is, and then you must believe it. What you deserve in life is up to you.

9. **Moments of Clarity:** Sometimes we don't need to question how we know the answers. The right path will reveal itself if you are willing to see it. Then it is up to you to jump the curb and roadblocks and go with the flow, not against it. Trust yourself because you know a whole lot more than you give yourself credit for.

10. **This Is It:** Understand who you really are and what your very unique and special gift is to this world, and then find a way to live it.

Life is made up of all kinds of moments. Moments of risk. Moments of happiness. Moments of clarity. Moments full of courage and fearlessness. The big question is whether we give ourselves credit when we actually have the opportunity to be aware of and enjoy some of these moments. How do we learn from them, grow from them, and understand how to live through these moments to power us forward?

We all know that life can be hard. But it can also be amazing. It is how you choose to live your life and what you choose to do with this information that make the real difference. Be strong. You do know who you are. Sometimes it just takes a little nudge, sometimes from an unexpected source, to help you remember what is important and to help make sure you are living the life you choose.

As my very wise ninety-five-year-old five-year-old said to me on the eve of her sixth birthday, "Being five was great. So many good memories!" So get out there and enjoy today and the moments there for the taking. There is no limit to the abundance available for each and every one of us who dares to whisper out loud what our dreams are and then take the steps to make them reality.

To reach the author regarding speaking engagement opportunities or for more information, you may reach her at info@kimberlynne.com.